T0068030

AN OBEDIENT DOG IS A HAPPY DOG

Train your dog to show quality in just 8 weeks

D.A. Wilson

authorHOUSE®

AuthorHouse™
1663 Liberty Drive
Bloomington, IN 47403
www.authorhouse.com
Phone: 1-800-839-8640

Published by AuthorHouse   03/02/2012

ISBN: 978-1-4685-5634-6 (sc)
ISBN: 978-1-4685-5635-3 (e)

This book is intended to assist a dog owner to teach his or her dog basic obedience with a few advanced features over an eight week period. Adhering to the instructions and scheduling in this book will assure any owner or handler that their dog will at least learn basic obedience and possibly reach show dog quality.

If you are participating in a structured obedience class, do not let this material interfere with your instructor's program.

I wish to acknowledge Megan Price and her dog, Barney for producing the picture representing Rowdy, who could have passed as Barney's twin brother

AN OBEDIENT DOG IS A HAPPY DOG

This work is dedicated to Rowdy, a Border Collie and his sidekick, Cherokee, who was a loving and gentle German Shepherd.

During seven obedience matches, Rowdy placed 4th once, 2nd once and 1st 5 times. Each of his first place finishes resulted from perfect scores of 200 points. Two of his perfect scores were achieved during outdoor matches, which is normally unheard of. His lowest score ever was 196.

Although Cherokee was a well trained and very obedient dog, she was never entered in obedience competition. Due to inattention and improper care on my part, Cherokee died due to heart worms.

Dedication is also made to Cheyenne, my most recent German Shepherd. Cheyenne, like Cherokee was gentle and loving, well behaved and obedient, and was my faithful companion for 12 years. After serving as a cancer research dog for the University of Cincinnati and being completely cured of cancer, Cheyenne had to be put down due to severe, crippling arthritis.

I also dedicate this work to K.C., a black Lab/Rottie mix, who we obtained when she was 1 year old. K.C. was never trained to show quality, but was a sweetheart, who behaved as a lady and returned our love for 3 years. Unfortunately, K.C. developed untreatable cancer and had to be put down at the tender age of four.

K.C.'s replacement, who is my present companion, is Tori, a lab/spaniel mix, who like K.C. is well behaved and loving and at the age of 12 is in good health and is at my side at this very moment.

To all my babies I say "thanks for the memories" and you'll be in my heart forever.

Sunnyvale, California
Revised February, 2012

Howdy, Rowdy

NOVICE DOG TRAINING
By D.A. Wilson

INTRODUCTION TO TRAINING

There are three basic phases of obedience training for dogs. They are Novice, Advanced and Utility Dog. Novice training is basic training, which is conducted on lead (leash) and covers such things as heel, sit, down, stay, wait and come. Advanced training covers the same commands without a lead and includes other exercises such as broad and high jumping and retrieving. Utility Dog training is extremely advanced and teaches the dog to follow directions by hand signals and to locate objects by scent, such as a particular dumb bell out of a group of dumb bells. The dog is sent to locate and retrieve over an obstacle course by following hand signals and silent commands.

You are about to embark on a new experience. New for you and new for your pet. You have to make it a team effort, and repetition and consistency are very important. Training should be conducted by <u>one handler</u>, until the novice training program has been completed. Then it would be advisable for other family members to participate, so that everyone in the family will be able to control the dog and the dog will learn to respond to commands of all family members.

A dog's formal training should start between the age of 4 months and 8 months. Ideally, 6 to 7 months of age. However, old dogs can learn new tricks, so do not let your dog's age hold you back. Only one or two new commands should be taught each week. Training sessions should last approximately 20 minutes. No less than 10 and no longer than 30 minutes per session. There should be one training session each week that extends to 45 or 50 minutes, during which all previous lessons should be reviewed. Training exercises should be conducted every day, <u>without fail</u>, regardless of the weather and in spite of any commitments you may have. If the weather is inclement, an indoor or protected area should be used. <u>Under no circumstances</u> should less than 10 minutes be devoted to training on any given day.

During the novice training program the handler should use a firm, crisp voice. It is not necessary to shout, but you want to keep the dog's attention and teach him to recognize that commands are just that, commands. Be careful that you do not give any inadvertent hand signals or other cues to the dog as you teach each exercise. That will come later.

Should you and your dog be attending a structured obedience class, do not let this material interfere with your instructor's program.

There are many good teaching methods, but too much advice from too many sources is worse than no advice at all.

Adhering to the guidelines presented in this book will assure that you and your dog will be successful in making your dog an OBEDIENT AND HAPPY DOG.

Good luck with your training program.

DISCIPLINE

Never, I repeat **"<u>NEVER</u>"** strike your dog. There is **<u>NO</u>** indiscretion severe enough to warrant striking and there are other methods that are more effective and less likely to cause injury to your dog, physically or mentally.

Do you get that? **"<u>NEVER</u>!"**

All discipline must be administered at the time of the indiscretion or your dog's short memory will prevent him from understanding what he is being punished for.

For minor indiscretions wrap your hand around the dog's snout and apply just enough pressure to maintain control of him. Place the palm on top of the snout and wrap your fingers into his mouth. DO NOT squeeze, as the mouth is very tender and you want to correct him without causing injury. With his snout firmly gripped in your hand, berate him with "Bad Boy!" or words of your own choosing. I prefer "MALO!", pronounced MA (as in mama) and LO (as in low). That is Spanish for "BAD".

Use of a foreign word is advisable, because your dog will not normally hear it during normal conversation and its meaning will have more impact when he does hear it. Once your dog learns the meaning of a scolding, you should be able to dispense with physical contact and simply correct him verbally.

For major indiscretions, such as chasing the paper buy or direct disobedience (its okay to chase the UPS man), grasp the fur and loose skin on each side of the dog's neck. Force him to look you in the eyes and scold him verbally. Be sure to keep your face at arm's length to assure that you don't get bit. Even the most loving and gentle dog may resent that method at first, so be careful, but remember, that is the best and preferred method for disciplining.

These forms of punishment cause the dog to realize that you are in control. They also instill a sense of shame in the dog, he knows that he has done wrong, but there is no chance that he will get injured. Also the dog will not develop a fear of you, your hand, a newspaper or any other object.

For the most outrageous indiscretions, grasp your dog by the fur and loose skin on each side of his neck, hold him at arm's length, protecting your face, and lift him upward until his front paws are off the ground. Then shake your hands forward and backward a couple of times while reprimanding him verbally, Maintain control of him and make him continue to look you in the eyes after you have stopped shaking him.

GETTING STARTED

In novice dog training we start out with a choker (choke chain) and a 6' leather or woven lead (leash). Some leashes are cute and/or dainty, but for training purposes, they are absolutely useless. Get something sturdy and do it right. In fact, it is not a leash, it is a lead. Therefore that is what I'm going to call it.

The choke chain should be placed over the dog's head so that one end of the chain passes under the left side of the dog's neck and the end that lies against the right side of the dog's neck passes downward through the ring that has passed under the neck. That is to insure that the choker releases when pressure is released by the handler. If the choker is placed on the dog's neck improperly, it may not release and may cause injury or discomfort to the dog.

Once you have placed the choker around your dog's neck, **leave it there.** He doesn't have much that he can call his own, so the choke chain should become his own personal jewelry.

Do not be afraid to jerk sharply on the lead as a corrective measure. If the choke chain has been properly applied, it will not hurt the dog.

When giving a moving command to a dog: heel, come, and fetch, etc., say the dog's name before giving the command. Example: "Rowdy, HEEL!" Hearing his name gets the dog's attention and he has no excuse for not hearing or heeding the command. When you give a sedentary command: sit, stay, wait, down, etc. DO NOT use the dog's name. This helps the dog to recognize a command that is going to require action on his part and a command that is going to require him to perform a sedentary or stationary task.

An important part of dog training is to teach your dog how to learn. Once he learns how to learn, teaching and learning can become fun instead of work. In the beginning both the handler and the dog should consider the training sessions as work sessions. There should be as few distractions as possible. Try to work in seclusion, so that you and the dog can concentrate on the matters at hand. There will be plenty of time to show off your dog later.

To help your dog distinguish between work sessions and play time or leisure time, use a release command at the end of each work session. Example: "No Mas!" The a is pronounced as "ah". That is Spanish for "no more". Use of a word or term like that will not be part of your normal conversation, so the dog only hears it at the end of a work session or other activity and recognizes it as his release command.

After giving the release command, slap your hands together, pat your dog on his side a couple of times or use some other playful gesture to assure that he realizes that the work session has ended. Once you have completed this training program you can also use the release command when you want to end a play session as well as a work session.

It is not necessary to use treats for training purposes. In fact, I recommend against it, The dog should learn to comply with your commands simply to satisfy his handler, and should derive self satisfaction from his own obedience. During training however, it is necessary to praise your dog for a job well done.

A few pats on the chest, just under the neck and verbal praise in the form of "Good Boy!" is treat enough. For example: if you are trying to get your dog to Stay, don't keep saying "Good Boy!" The dog will think that the exercise is over. Reinforce the dog during the exercise by repeating the command, "Stay", but do it in a gentle, more reminding voice than when the command was originally given. Once the dog has complied with a command, praise him graciously.

WEEK ONE

The first exercise is HEEL. When a dog heels he can be walking or sitting at the handler's left. **NEVER** <u>allow your dog to walk at your right side</u>. Should you find it necessary to jerk the leash, the choke chain may not release and injury or discomfort to the dog can occur. Besides, you want to be as consistent as possible, so let's keep the dog to the left and the master to the right.

By the time you start this program, you will probably have taught your dog to sit. If you have, it will make it easier to teach him to heel. If not, teach heeling and sitting together.

Start out by holding the loose end of the leach in your right hand. Take up the excess lead and hold it in your right hand, as well. Feed out enough lead so that there is no slack when your right hand is placed at your belt buckle. DO NOT grasp the lead with your left hand. You'll need your left hand for other things.

Give the command, "NAME, HEEL!" Then immediately step out, LEFT FOOT FIRST and gently jerk on the lead in a forward motion. Continue jerking and releasing as necessary to get the dog moving. Walk a few paces and then stop. Stop on the LEFT FOOT FIRST, and then bring the right foot along side. Jerk lightly to stop the dog.

Then apply pressure to the dog's back, just ahead of the tail and between the hips. Press downward with your left hand and upward with the lead.

This will seem awkward at first, but will become natural with practice. The idea is to get the dog to automatically sit at your left side with his front paws even with the tips of your toes each time you stop. Do not concern yourself with form during the first few weeks. You can work on positioning later. Each week you should concentrate on the form for the previous exercise. Originally you should get the dog to understand that when you are walking with him, he is to walk to your left, abreast and with his shoulders relatively close to your left leg. When you stop, the dog should sit to your left, facing forward. There will be more on heeling form in this chapter. Heeling is taught first, because during training, most other stationary commands will be given from that position.

As your dog learns to heel, he will probably resist sitting when you come to a stop. You must be persistent. Give the command "Sit!" and push downward on the hind quarters while pulling upward with the lead. DO NOT use the dog's name when you give the "Sit!" command.

If your dog is of a size that will permit it, you can cross your right foot behind your left leg and tap downward with the tip of your right shoe. Tap, don't kick. We don't want to hurt the dog, just startle him.

At first he will wonder where that blow came from. He will soon learn to anticipate it and as a result he will begin sitting to avoid that annoying contact. Whenever you come to a stop and the dog sits, either voluntarily or with help, praise him and pat his chest. When you are done with a work session, give the release command.

When heeling your dog, change directions often. Turns to the right or left should be done in military fashion, pivoting on your left foot if you are turning right and pivoting on the right foot if your are turning left. To do a "to the rear", pivot on your left foot twice. This is going to be very confusing to your dog for several days and you will have to help him by giving the "Name, Heel!" command as you make each change of direction and jerk on the lead in the direction of the turn, both as you start and as you negotiate the turn.

If your dog does not seem to respond, jerk harder. If the choke chain is applied properly, it will not hurt the dog. At first, when you make a left turn, you will bump into the dog and visa versa. That's okay.

Take advantage of that situation and use your left knee to bump his right shoulder. As he learns to anticipate the bump, he will begin turning to avoid contact. After 3 or 4 days, start changing your gait. Break into a trot for a few yards then resume walking.

Each time you change your gait or direction, give the "Name, Heel!" command and a reminding jerk on the lead. As the dog learns to comply you can gradually eliminate the jerking of the lead and you can eventually eliminate the verbal command.

The proper position for the dog during a heeling exercise is for the dog to be to the handler's left, abreast, with his right shoulder close to the left leg of the handler and slightly ahead of the leg or even with it. When stopped in the heeling position, the dog should be sitting erect, facing forward with his front paws even with the tips of the handler's shoes. It can be expected that an enthusiastic dog will sneak an inquiring glance toward the handler's face once in awhile. This is good, because it shows that he is interested in what he is doing and he wants to please.

WEEK TWO

The second week you should continue the heeling exercise and begin teaching your dog to SIT on command, whether he is at your side or elsewhere. Teaching a dog to sit is done by giving the "SIT!" command. Remember; do not use the dog's name when giving the "SIT!" command or any other sedentary or stationary command. As you give the command to sit, press down on the hind quarters with your left hand, while pulling upward on the lead with your right hand. When the dog does sit either voluntarily or with help praise him and pat the chest. Continue the Sit command when performing the heeling exercise. He should learn to sit automatically when you come to a stop. When this begins to happen, you can quit giving the verbal command.

During the second week add some variety to the heeling exercise. Set up two chairs or two volunteers (chairs are best for starters) and place them approximately 6 to 8 feet apart. Perform the heeling exercise while doing figure eights around and between the obstacles. Stop and sit your dog occasionally as you perform the exercise and change directions every few cycles. Ideally, during the 4th week and beyond, the obstacles would be two individuals, each with their own dog sitting in the heeling position at their handler's side. A jerk on the lead will discourage distractions.

During the second week you will also teach your dog to Stay. There is a difference between STAY and WAIT. Don't get them confused or the dog will get confused also.

If you want your dog to remain in position until you return to the heeling position you will command him to "STAY!". If you intend to call him to you, use the "WAIT!" command. For the time being, concentrate on staying.

From the HEEL position, with your dog sitting to your left side, give the command "STAY!" Do not use the dog's name. Step off with your <u>right foot</u>, then turn to your left and face your dog. If the dog fails to stay, repeat the command "STAY!", push downward on the hind quarters with your left hand and pull upward on the lead with your right hand. Get him back into the sitting, heeling position and command him to "STAY!" Encourage him to stay by saying "STAY" over and over again, but not in a commanding voice.

Back up slowly until you reach the end of the lead. Continue saying "STAY" as you back up and even after you have reached the end of the lead. After a few seconds, advance toward your dog and walk past his left side and around behind him to the heeling position. Hesitate for a 3 count, then praise and pat your dog. Repeat the exercise.

The dog MUST remain in the sitting position throughout the exercise in order for it to have been performed properly. As the dog gets the idea, let out more lead (get a longer one if you wish) until you are standing as far away from your dog as possible.

During the second week of this exercise, drop the lead when you reach the end of it and try working up to a distance of approximately 15 feet. As you progress, extend the time that you are facing your dog to at least 3 minutes, before returning to him.

NEVER call your dog after you have given the STAY command, unless it is absolutely necessary. Return to him and release him properly. Should you anticipate calling him from a commanded position, use the WAIT command in lieu of the STAY command.

Don't forget, when he does it right, either voluntarily or with help, praise and pat.

REMEMBER: STAY means STAY (I'm not going to call you). WAIT means that I am going to call you from that position.

Continue to work on heeling FORM.

WEEK THREE

During the third week, continue the previous week's exercises and start a new lesson, the "DOWN!" command. Again we do not use the dog's name when giving a sedentary or stationary command. Start in the sitting position. Shorten up on the lead so that your right hand is just a few inches from the choke chain. Give the command "DOWN!" and tug firmly on the lead with your right hand. Keep repeating the command and tugging downward until the dog lies down.

You don't want him flopping over on his side, but lying on his belly. If he rolls onto his side, physically roll him back into the proper position. If the dog wants to lie on his side while he's napping, that's fine. Just don't let him do it while he is working. Incidentally, your dog should NEVER lie on his side during any exercise activity.

As the dog complies with the command, either voluntarily or with help, PAT and PRAISE. Spend a few minutes at a time going from sit to down, practice heeling for a few minutes then return to the DOWN exercise. Never give your dog the "DOWN!" command while he is walking in the HEEL position. Have him sit before going down from the heeling position.

Remember: At the end of each work session, give the release command and romp with your dog for a few seconds. That can be limited to slapping your hands together in a playful manner and giving him a few pats on the side or back.

If you want the dog to SIT or DOWN, go ahead and give him the command, or you can release the dog to go about his own business. The dog MUST learn that you will be giving him commands at times other than during work sessions, so do not hesitate to give commands when you feel it necessary or when you get the urge.

ALWAYS complete a successful HEEL exercise of at least 2 or 3 steps before giving the release command. In other words ALWAYS end the work session with the heeling exercise.

Once your dog gets the idea of what DOWN means, start giving him the command from a distance. ALWAYS make sure he obeys. That may require you to get up, cross the room or yard and help him, so don't give him the command unless you are willing to do your part.

WEEK FOUR

You should be continuing with all previous exercises, and by now your dog should be complying with the "SIT, STAY!" command. Do not go beyond this point until you are satisfied with his performance. Continue performing the previous exercises until you and your dog have reasonably mastered them.

Up to this point you have not called your dog from a stationary position. At least, I hope that you haven't. Once again, NEVER call your dog once you have given him the STAY command. Think ahead. If you anticipate calling him from the sit or down position, give him the WAIT command rather than the STAY command. If your dog has reasonably learned to STAY on command, you can begin to teach him to WAIT.

Remember, when you had your dog HEEL, you stepped off with your left foot and when you had your dog STAY, you stepped off with your right foot first. We will again step off with the right foot following the WAIT command. From the heeling position, give the "WAIT!" command and step off with the right foot. Turn left and face your dog, making sure that he remains in the sitting position, then back up a few steps, feeding out the lead as you back up. If the dog breaks from the sitting position, say "NO!" and correct his position and start to retreat again.

It is not necessary to start from the heeling position if the dog breaks from the sitting position, just continue from where you were, but repeat the command "WAIT!" as you make corrections and as you retreat.

The following addition to this exercise should not be introduced until your dog is performing to your satisfaction.

After you have retreated a few feet and with the dog WAITING, give the command "NAME,

COME!" Jerk gently on the lead and guide the dog toward you. You can even back up a few more feet as the dog gets nearer.

When you have reeled in most of the lead, stop in place, give the command "SIT!" and guide the dog into a sitting position by lifting the lead upward with your right hand and, if necessary, by pressing downward on the hind quarters. Again, form is not an issue at first, but you will need to work on form as the dog gets the idea of what he is supposed to be doing.

The perfect performance of the Wait, Come exercise is for the dog and handler to be in the sitting, heeling position. The handler gives the "WAIT!" command and steps off with his right foot. The dog remains in the sitting position. The handler turns left twice and stands, facing the dog. The dog remains in the sitting position for a reasonable length of time then the handler gives the "NAME, COME!" command. The dog advances toward the handler and sits in front of him with his toes touching or almost touching the tips of the handler's shoes. The dog faces upward toward the handler's face.

The handler waits for a 3 or 4 count then walks past the dog's left side and circles around to the heeling position. The handler then gives the "NAME, HEEL!" command and steps off with his left foot. After just a few steps, the handler gives the release command and pats and praises his dog.

Repeat the exercise or terminate the session.

WEEK FIVE

During the fifth week continue each of the previous week's exercises and add a little to the WAIT, COME exercise. That addition is to drop the lead when you are facing your dog and back up a little at a time before calling your dog. Work back to approximately 15 feet by the end of the week. After your dog gets to you and sits, pick up the lead and circle back to the HEEL position.

Also during the fifth week you will start teaching your dog to STAND and STAY. From the HEELING position, give the "HEEL!" command, step off with your left foot and immediately give the "STAND!" command. The dog will think, "What the heck does that mean?" Show him. Apply upward tension on the lead with your right hand and place your left hand under the dog's body, just ahead of the rear legs and hold him there. Then command, "STAY!" Back away to the end of the lead while repeating the word STAY in a reminding tone. If the dog starts to move, step back to him, reapply upward tension on the lead and place your left hand back under his body and repeat the "STAY!" command. Then back away again. Continue to repeat the exercise a few times, but don't overtax the dog. Remember to end the exercise by stepping off from the HEELING position before giving the release command.

Standing and Staying should always be followed by a HEELING repetition. It is okay to pat and praise your dog while he is STANDING and STAYING, but NEVER release your dog from the STANDING position.

In subsequent weeks, as your dog is learning to STAND and STAY, begin applying downward pressure on his hind quarters. Lightly at first and with moderate force later on. We want the dog to STAND with his weight evenly distributed on all fours and firmly planted in place.

Also do little things to annoy the dog while he is standing. Let children run by or make noise or scuff your feet or make clucking sounds. Drill this exercise into him until he remains in the STANDING position in spite of your activities or other distractions.

WHY? If you ever show your dog in obedience trials, the judge will be checking firmness of the dog's stance by applying pressure to the hind quarters. The dog MUST not move. That's a sure way to drop 20 points immediately.

WEEK SIX

The sixth week is a review of the previous five weeks. Congratulations, you've come a long way in a very short time. You must be proud of your dog, I am. Continue to repeat all exercises. By this time your dog should be very accustomed to the "STAY!" command from the sitting position. We now want to start working on DOWN and DOWN, STAY. Start from the HEELING position and command your dog to "DOWN!" <u>DO NOT use his name</u>. Give the "STAY!" command and step off with your right foot. Turn around and face your dog and repeat the steps used when teaching your dog to SIT, STAY back in the second and third weeks.

Gradually increase the distance from your dog to approximately 25 feet before returning to him and after the fourth or fifth day try to completely remove yourself from view. Step behind a tree, walk around the corner of a building or leave the room. Sneak a peek at your dog to confirm that he is STAYING in the DOWN position. If he moves or sits, immediately return to your dog and physically correct him while repeating "DOWN, STAY!" Keep at it until he gets it right.

When you have reached a point where you leave your dog in the DOWN position and he will stay there with you out of sight, gradually increase the out of sight time to five minutes and the SIT, STAY to 3 minutes. You do not have to get out of sight during the SIT, STAY exercise, just move about 20 to 25 feet away.

Remember, the exercise is not complete until YOU have returned to the HEELING position, stepped out and patted and praised your dog.

During this week you should teach your dog to FINISH from the COME, SIT position. Apply the lead and start from the SITTING, HEELING position. Have your dog WAIT and step away from him, Right Foot First. Assume a position where you are facing your dog with the lead extended. Call your dog to you. When he stops and sits facing you with his toes aligned to your tocs, hesitate for a 3 or 4 count. Next, command your dog to "NAME, HEEL!" "WHAT?" Command your dog to "NAME, HEEL!" and use the lead to guide him around to his right (your left). The dog should start out to his right making a counter clockwise circle, ending up in the HEELING position alongside your left leg. Of course, when he gets to the HEELING position he should SIT. As the dog learns to FINISH, he will most likely start doing it in a rather quick fashion and may even develop his own snappy technique. Some dogs literally spin and almost jump into the HEELING position.

This can become one of your dog's showiest moves.

WEEK SEVEN

We are now at week seven. You're almost there. You have a fairly well behaved dog, you should be feeling quite satisfied and you have probably been showing off your dog. If you haven't, you should be. It is now time for distractions. I don't mean yelling and running around, but just having people around doing what they normally do.

STAND you dog and let someone apply pressure to the hind quarters. Have the person approach the dog, offer the back of their hand to the dog's nose, then gradually move the hand onto the dog's head and stroke the fur back to hind quarters. Then apply gentle pressure downward. If the dog does not cooperate make the proper corrections and repeat the exercise. The dog MUST become receptive to such treatment.

Week seven is also the time for refinement of all previous exercises. Review each exercise and make sure that your form and that of the dog is up to snuff. If it isn't, concentrate on those elements. Review the entire written program and go through each step with the dog.

While you and your dog are reviewing the program, you can start teaching hand signals.

Hand signals are not usually taught or used during Novice training and if you show your dog in Novice competition, you will not be permitted to use them. You will have to use verbal commands ONLY and will be penalized for using hand signals or any other physical prompts.

I believe however, that this is the proper time to start with hand signals. The dog is in the learning mode and it adds some variety to the program for both the dog and the handler.

Remember when you were instructed to step off with your left foot when you wanted your dog to accompany you and to step off with your right foot when you wanted the dog to STAY or WAIT? You were already teaching silent commands, you just didn't know it. Hopefully, the dog picked up on the left foot, right foot business. Try it. Assume the HEELING position. Step off with your left foot and see if the dog HEELS along. If not, give a gentle tug on the lead end encourage him to follow. If you need to encourage him verbally, do so, but in a reminding voice, not a crisp, firm command. Work on that.

Next assume the SITTING, HEELING position and step off with your right foot. Does Fido STAY? If not, start again.

Step off with the right foot and give the verbal reminder to STAY. It may take some extra effort, but with verbal reminders to HEEL, STAY or WAIT, you should be able to teach your dog to HEEL when you step off with your left foot and to STAY or WAIT when you step off with your right foot.

I had a problem with this until I decided to flash the palm of my left hand in front of my dog's face when I wanted him to STAY and reached across my body with the palm of my right hand flashing past the dog's face when I wanted him to WAIT. Once I started doing that, Rowdy caught on very quickly.

By now your dog should know how to HEEL and how to STAY or WAIT, so it's just a matter of getting the dog to associate the difference between a left foot start and a right foot start. As your dog becomes familiar with these commands and their differences, Walk with your dog from the start position and after a few steps, flash you left hand in front of his face to get him to STAND for inspection. He should stop in place and assume the inspection stance. Again, this is going to take extra effort on your part, but remember that you want to show off.

Once more, it is extremely important that you end each exercise session with a step off from the SITTING, HEELING position, followed by Pat and Praise.

WEEK EIGHT

Week eight brings us to the final silent commands. Continue to work on all previous exercises, with and without hand signals and start on the remaining silent commands. By now you should be learning to teach and your dog should be learning to learn, so from this point on you should have very few problems, if any.

With your dog in front of you in the COME, SIT position (the dog is directly in front of you and looking up) place your left hand on your abdomen, just below the belt line, with your palm facing your body. Snap your left hand to a position beside your left leg and give the "NAME, HEEL!" command. Your dog should do a little pirouette into the SITING, HEELING position. If not, guide him around as you did when you taught him to FINISH.

Eventually, the flip of your hand alone should be command enough to get your dog to FINISH.

For the hand signal to SIT, simply place your right hand in front of your abdomen, just below the belt line. Crisply point to the ground just to the right and slightly ahead of your right leg; and give the "SIT!" command. Don't use his name, Your dog should know the "SIT!" command by now and it is just a matter getting him to associate the hand signal with the command.

Combine the hand signal with the verbal command for a couple of days, then try the hand signal by itself. Don't forget to Pat and Praise.

The hand signal for DOWN consists of raising your right hand as though taking an oath. Give the "DOWN!" command and crisply drop your right hand to a position along side of your right leg as though you were snapping to attention. Again, your dog should know the meaning of the "DOWN!" command and it is simply a matter of getting him to associate the hand signal with the command.

The final hand signal is "COME!" With your dog facing you from 15 to 20 feet away, extend your right hand straight out about shoulder high. Place your palm down with your fingers pointing in the general direction of the dog. Give the verbal "NAME, COME!" command and crisply bend your right elbow so the inside of your right hand snaps to your left shoulder area. Try the hand signal with the verbal command then try the hand signal by itself. Be patient, although your dog is now a good student, don't overtax his relatively small brain. At this point, PATIENCE is the name of the game.

As your dog become proficient with hand signals, begin combining hand signals. Get him to WAIT, walk about 30 feet away. Turn and face your dog.

Hesitate for a 5 count then give the COME hand signal. As soon as he breaks to approach you, give the DOWN hand signal. Almost immediately give the COME hand signal. Continue until he reaches the COME, SIT position and is sitting in front of you, looking up. Hesitate then give the FINISH hand signal. Step out, then PAT and Praise.

Eight long, hard weeks have ended. What do you have to show for your efforts? You have learned a lot and so has your dog. As a team you should be able to HEEL, SIT, lay DOWN, STAY, WAIT, COME, finish to the HEEL position and STAND and STAY for inspection.

Besides performing each of these exercises, you should be well on your way to full compliance to hand signals.

Show off your dog at every opportunity. You will enjoy it and so will your dog. At this time you should make it a family affair. Your dog should learn to obey every member of your HIS family and all family members should learn to work with the dog.

If you have any opportunity to enter your dog in obedience trials, do so. It is the thrill of a life time when you win best of show or even a lesser prize.

As I stated before "There are many good teaching methods, but too much advice from too many sources is worse than no advice at all."

Hopefully, you have found this training manual to not only be productive and educational, but entertaining and rewarding. I also hope that you have enjoyed observing these instructions as much as I have composing them.

All correspondence e-mailed to dawson322@ att.net will be acknowledged. Your comments and results would be greatly appreciated.

Best of Show

Printed in the United States
By Bookmasters